We Are One

The Story of Bayard Rustin

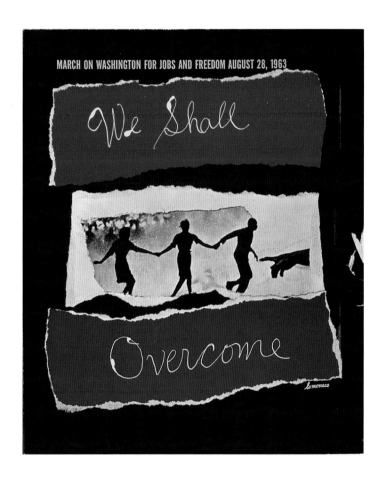

Larry Dane Brimner

CALKINS CREEK

HONESDALE, PENNSYLVANIA

Library of Congress Cataloging-in-Publication Data

Brimner, Larry Dane.
  We are one : the story of Bayard Rustin / Larry Dane Brimner. — 1st ed.
    48 p. : ill. ; 27 x 29 cm.
Summary: Captures a story of passion, courage, and triumph through Bayard's own words
and archival photographs, and through spirituals and protest songs that Bayard often sang.
  ISBN 978-1-59078-498-3
  [1. Rustin, Bayard, 1912-1987—Juvenile literature. 2. Rustin, Bayard, 1912-1987.
3. Rustin, Bayard, 1912-1987. 4. Civil rights workers—United States—Biography—Juvenile
literature. 5. African Americans—Civil rights—Juvenile literature. 6. African Americans—
Biography—Juvenile literature. 7. Civil rights movements—United States—History—20th
century—Juvenile literature. 8. Civil rights workers. 9. African Americans—Biography.
10. African Americans—Civil rights. 11. Civil rights—United States—Biography. 12. African
Americans—Civil rights. 13. African Americans—Biography.] I. Title.

2007299437

CALKINS CREEK
An Imprint of Boyds Mills Press, Inc.
815 Church Street
Honesdale, Pennsylvania 18431

First edition
The text of this book is set in 13-point Sabon.

10 9 8 7 6 5

Picture Sources

AP/Wide World Photos: 35, 41.

Chester County Historical Society, West Chester, PA: 7 (bottom).

© Wally McNamee/CORBIS: 5; © Bettmann/CORBIS: 31.

Estate of Bayard Rustin: 7 (top), 9, 14, 15, 16, 17, 20, 21, 25, 27, 29, 32, 33, 36, 44 (top
inset), 46 (right), 47 (left and right), 48 (right).

Leonard McCombe, photographer/Time & Life Pictures/Getty Images: 48 (left).

Library of Congress Prints and Photographs Division, LC-USZC4-6525, Louis LoMonaco,
artist: 1; Library of Congress Prints and Photographs Division, LC-USZ62-24132:
11 (bottom); Library of Congress Prints and Photographs Division, LC-USZ62-83902:
22; Library of Congress Prints and Photographs Division, LC-USZ62-120351, Danny
Lyon, photographer: 39; Library of Congress Prints and Photographs Division, LC-USZ62-
133369, Orlando Fernandez, photographer: 40; Library of Congress Prints and Photographs
Division, LC-USZ62-118986: 46 (left).

National Archives: 11 (top), 19, 42, 43, 44 (center), 45, endpapers.

General Research & Reference Division, Schomburg Center for Research in Black Culture,
The New York Public Library, Astor, Lenox and Tilden Foundations: 10, 12 (left), 13 (left);
Manuscripts, Archives and Rare Books Division, Schomburg Center for Research in Black
Culture, The New York Public Library, Astor, Lenox and Tilden Foundations: 12 (right);
Photographs and Prints Division, Schomburg Center for Research in Black Culture,
The New York Public Library, Astor, Lenox, and Tilden Foundations, John Vachon,
photographer: 13 (right).

Source Notes

Page 13
"tiresome" . . . "indigestion": Bayard Rustin, interview by Ed Edwin, November 14, 1984, "The
Reminiscences of Bayard Rustin," transcript, Columbia University Oral History Research Office, p. 1–3.

Page 17
"[T]he Communists appeared . . .": Bayard Rustin, *Strategies for Freedom: The Changing Patterns
of Black Protest* (New York: Columbia University Press, 1976), p. 9.

Page 23
"Why . . .": Bayard Rustin, "Nonviolence vs. Jim Crow," in *Down the Line: The Collected
Writings of Bayard Rustin* (Chicago: Quadrangle Books, 1971), p. 5.

Page 24
"There is no need . . .": Bayard Rustin, "Nonviolence vs. Jim Crow," in *Time on Two Crosses:
    The Collected Writings of Bayard Rustin*, ed. Devon W. Carbado and Donald Weise
    (San Francisco: Cleis Press, 2003), p. 3.
"from one to another . . .": Ibid., p. 4.
"*Mister* Rustin.": Ibid., p. 5.

Page 26
"the basis of continuous violence.": Bayard Rustin, "Letter to the Draft Board," in *Time on
    Two Crosses*, p. 12.
"from the basic spiritual truth . . .": Ibid., p. 11.
"which separates man . . .": Ibid., p. 12.
"Though joyfully following . . .": Ibid., p. 13.

Page 28
"Well, you see, . . .": Rustin, "Reminiscences," September 12, 1985, p. 292.

Page 33
"Negroes were thrilled . . .": Bayard Rustin, "Montgomery Diary," in *Time on Two Crosses*, p. 59.

Page 37
"I ask of you . . .": Bayard Rustin, "To the Evergreen Tree," in *The Garnet and White*, West
Chester, PA: West Chester Public High School, April 1932, Volume XXIV, no. 5, p. 8.

Page 42
"Gentlemen, everything is . . .": Bayard Rustin, *Brother Outsider: The Life of Bayard Rustin*,
DVD, directed by Nancy Kates and Bennett Singer (San Francisco: Independent Television
Service, 2002).

Page 45
"one of those few moments . . .": Rustin, "Reminiscences," May 8, 1985, p. 216.

Page 46
"We are all one. . . .": Rustin, *Brother Outsider: The Life of Bayard Rustin*.

To the promise that America has yet to keep
—L.D.B.

FOR A SUMMER MORNING IN WASHINGTON, D.C.,

the day dawned clear and mercifully cool.

It was Wednesday, August 28, 1963,

and Bayard thought he would stroll to the Washington Monument to see how the march was shaping up. Less than eight weeks earlier, he had promised journalists and black leaders that he would deliver one hundred thousand protesters to the March on Washington for Jobs and Freedom—protesters united to voice their grievances against a government that had failed them. If everything went according to his plan, it would be the largest mass protest in the history of the United States. If everything went according to his plan, it would be a day to remember and a day the nation could not ignore.

Everything hinged on *if*.

When he reached the monument, Bayard looked around the grassy slopes that surround it. Journalists and members of the security patrol outnumbered the demonstrators! Then someone asked where the promised crowds were . . . and Bayard felt his stomach knot.

Early on the morning of August 28, 1963, the crowd around the Washington Monument was sparse.

FROM THE VERY BEGINNING it seemed that Bayard had been facing obstacles—and overcoming them. Julia Rustin had said she was going to let Bayard's mother raise him. But his mother was herself just a child—a teenager who was not prepared to care for an infant. One day, however, Julia looked into Bayard's crib and he smiled up at her. Then and there she decided to adopt the infant and raise him proper. Eight other children lived in her household, so there would be plenty of hands to help. And Bayard Taylor Rustin enchanted them all.

Eleven years later, in 1923, Bayard learned his family's secret: "Ma" Rustin—Julia—was really his grandmother. The "sister" he knew as Florence was really his mother.

Sometimes I feel like a motherless child

Sometimes I feel like a motherless child

Sometimes I feel like a motherless child

A long ways from home

A long ways from home.

Julia "Ma" Rustin strongly influenced Bayard's beliefs in pacifism and the equality of each individual before God.

The Vacation Bible School, here at the Gay Street Elementary School, was one of Julia's many pet projects, and Bayard (second row, second from left) was one of its frequent attendees.

THE LESSONS THAT BAYARD'S GRANDPARENTS taught him shaped the man he would become, and he carried these lessons with him the rest of his life.

His grandfather, Janifer Rustin, had been born into slavery during the last year of the Civil War. Lincoln's Emancipation Proclamation had freed the slaves in the South, but it did nothing to help blacks in the North, and Janifer Rustin was born in the North—in Maryland. He wouldn't be "free" until a year later, when the U.S. Congress passed the Thirteenth Amendment to the Constitution.

By the time Bayard was school-age, Janifer was providing the Rustin clan with a spacious, ten-room house in a racially mixed area in the east end of West Chester, Pennsylvania. His work as a steward at the Elks Lodge and caterer of parties for well-to-do white families meant that sometimes he brought home fancy delicacies like turtle soup, lobster Newburg, and the finest pâtés and cheeses. The Rustins were not rich. Oh—but sometimes they dined as if they were!

It was Janifer who taught Bayard the value and dignity of hard work. It was Julia, though, who was his moral compass. She had been raised in the Quaker faith—the Religious Society of Friends—and passed on its strong beliefs: that each person is a member of one family and equal before God, to live a life of nonviolence, and to treat everyone with love and respect. Bayard learned to live these lessons—sometimes the hard way. When he was in fifth grade, he and a group of his young white friends taunted the owner of a Chinese laundry with a racist chant. When Julia heard about it, she made Bayard spend his after-school time over the next two weeks in the laundry, washing and ironing. It was a lesson about prejudice that he never forgot.

Taylor

Nº 10 W. Gay St.
West Chester, Pa.

Janifer Rustin gained his freedom with the passage of the Thirteenth Amendment to the U.S. Constitution and moved from Maryland to West Chester in the 1880s.

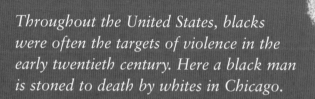

Throughout the United States, blacks were often the targets of violence in the early twentieth century. Here a black man is stoned to death by whites in Chicago.

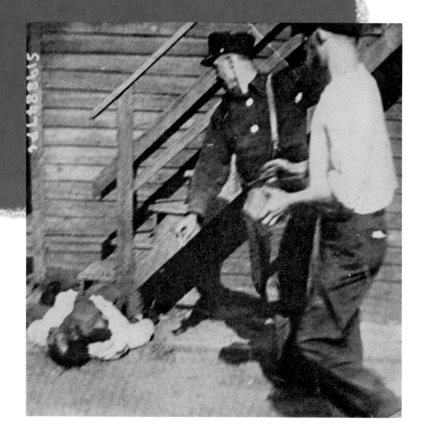

THE RUSTIN HOUSE WAS almost always a hubbub of activity. For the children and their friends, it was a neighborhood gathering place. Janifer had a generous nature, and Julia's Quaker beliefs made the house friendly and hospitable—a place where Bayard's many white friends were welcome even though social customs dictated that he typically was prohibited from entering their homes. Moreover, Julia belonged to several civic and civil rights organizations, including the National Association for the Advancement of Colored People (NAACP)—which she joined shortly after it was formed in 1909.

In the South following the Civil War, laws were passed to prevent blacks from voting, and throughout the United States, Negroes were discriminated against as a way to keep them from enjoying the benefits of freedom. The NAACP was formed to legally challenge those voting laws and other forms of discrimination that blacks faced in their daily lives. And it was Julia who provided NAACP members with friendly, comfortable lodging whenever they were in town. It wasn't that West Chester had no lodging for travelers; it was just that the lodging it offered was for whites only. It wasn't unusual for Ma and Pa to hustle Bayard and the other children out of their beds in the middle of the night so that W. E. B. Du Bois, a founding father of the NAACP and the first black person to earn a doctoral degree from Harvard University, would have a place to sleep when he was in town to lecture. The family also hosted other equally sophisticated and well-educated visitors, including James Weldon Johnson, a celebrated writer, and Mary McLeod Bethune, a distinguished educator. Johnson visited West

JIM CROW AND SEGREGATION

"Jim Crow" was not a real person but a popular nineteenth-century minstrel song. Performed by a white singer, face painted with black cork to resemble a black man, the routine was a silly, demeaning imitation of Negro singing and dancing. It's unclear how the minstrel song became synonymous with the laws of racial segregation that swept the South after the Civil War, but it did. By 1900, laws that required blacks to sit in the back of buses or to ride in black-only train cars or to attend black-only schools or to drink from black-only drinking fountains or to be buried in black sections of cemeteries were known as Jim Crow laws.

Blacks in the North had it a little better than those in the South. Many northern cities and towns had no Jim Crow laws. But just the same, there was a custom of social separation based on race. Discrimination whether by Jim Crow laws or by custom was commonplace throughout the United States. It was a way to isolate blacks in order to deprive them of social and economic advancement. The Emancipation Proclamation had ended slavery, but had it freed the slaves?

Chester on NAACP business; Bethune came to raise money for a school for Negro girls in Florida. And during their visits, Bayard heard their whispered conversations about lynchings of blacks in the South and Jim Crow laws that kept Negroes segregated, or separated, from whites, and so many troubles—so many troubles—despite the Emancipation.

The stories made Bayard's heart ache. Why didn't people treat each other with respect and dignity? Didn't they know that everyone was equal before God?

Top: Minstrel shows were a popular form of entertainment during the late 1800s and early 1900s. Their depictions of Negroes were usually demeaning and silly. Originally, white comedians performed in "black face," but Negroes also donned "black face" to entertain audiences. Bottom: A poster advertising comedian Billy Van and his "black face" persona.

Nobody knows de trouble I've seen

Nobody knows de trouble but Jesus

Nobody knows de trouble I've seen

Glory Hallelujah!

Following the Civil War, blacks migrated out of the South to escape violence.

OTHER, LESS FORTUNATE TRAVELERS stayed with the Rustins, too. The Civil War had left the South in economic ruin. Plantations were unproductive without slaves to work the fields. Other kinds of jobs were few, and those that existed were filled by whites, many of whom felt that the newly freed slaves threatened their livelihoods and way of life. These whites encouraged their legislators to pass laws that deprived blacks of their equality, and when those laws were challenged or struck down, some of these same white citizens turned to violence—often lynching, or hanging, those who challenged them. West Chester had been well known to blacks as a stop on the Underground Railroad during slave times—its Quaker population made it so. In the 1920s and 1930s the city became a refuge for people fleeing Jim Crow and the hopeless economic conditions and brutality in the South. Often, they made their way to the North with little more than the clothes on their backs.

AN AMERICAN REIGN OF TERROR

The Civil War may have ended in 1865, but it signaled the start of a reign of terror against blacks. In part because blacks were thrust suddenly into the labor force where they competed against whites for jobs, some whites felt threatened. The Ku Klux Klan (KKK) was formed at the end of the war by several white Confederate veterans. It quickly adopted violence as a method to intimidate blacks—and any whites who offered to help or support them—and spread rapidly throughout the South and, to a lesser extent, the rest of the United States.

The Ku Klux Klan instituted mob violence as a way to intimidate blacks and those who supported them. This engraving, published in 1897, depicts the lynching of an entire Tennessee family for no known offense.

Wearing white sheets and hoods that usually concealed their identities, Klansmen (and Klanswomen) broke up black prayer meetings, raided black homes, and ran out of town those schoolteachers who dared to teach blacks. Trying to control the political and economic lives of blacks, the Klan often turned to lynching—or hanging—to retaliate and intimidate. Lynching victims were men, women, and children, mostly black. They numbered in the thousands and were lynched for things as trivial as having a bad reputation, throwing stones, speaking to or insulting a white person, trying to vote, or simply being unpopular. In 1912, the year Bayard was born, some sixty-two lynchings of black Americans were recorded.

The Ku Klux Klan in costume, circa 1906–1907.

Bayard was struck by their poverty. Things he took for granted—running water, indoor plumbing, and gas lighting—were unfamiliar and strange to many of the visitors. He wished they could have a better life.

Bayard knew about white intolerance. Although there were no Jim Crow laws in West Chester, there was segregation just the same. Restaurants wouldn't serve him, or they would pack his food and tell him to take it with him. He could not try on clothes at the local store or use its public restroom. When he went to the movie house, he couldn't sit where he wanted. He had to sit in the seats reserved for colored. And his elementary school was for black children. White children went elsewhere. When Bayard asked Julia about these things, she cautioned him not to let his heart fill with hate. Hate, she explained, was a "tiresome" thing. Instead of getting "indigestion" over who did what to whom, she encouraged him to use his mind and talents to find solutions.

Segregation was commonplace throughout the United States into the mid-twentieth century. Blacks were forced to attend separate schools, use separate drinking fountains and restrooms, and sit in sections of theaters and waiting rooms reserved for "colored."

AND FIND SOLUTIONS IS WHAT HE DID.

By the time he started attending West Chester's integrated (and only) high school at the end of the 1920s, Bayard was already finding solutions to things that bothered him, with Julia and Janifer encouraging him to do what his heart told him he must.

He sat on the main floor of West Chester's Warner Theater, where blacks were not allowed to sit.

And he was arrested.

When the football team played a game that required the players to stay overnight, he started a rebellion. He told the coach that he and his black teammates would not participate in the game unless they were moved into the same accommodations that the white players had.

And they were moved.

He couldn't visit his best friend's house because his best friend, who was white, lived with an aunt who didn't welcome Negroes in her home. So Bayard decided they should meet at the library.

It was neutral ground.

Bayard was a likable and gifted athlete whose opponents said he would quote them lines of poetry following a tackle.

A high-school education was rare during the Great Depression of the 1930s when money and jobs were scarce and desperation was plentiful. Many young people, if they reached high school at all, dropped out in the first or second year to try to scratch out a living. This was especially true of blacks, who often viewed high school as a useless endeavor. Why go to high school when so many job opportunities, even when they existed, were automatically shut tight to blacks? But Bayard was different. Not only did he complete high school, a singular achievement in 1932, but he graduated near the top of his class.

Although most of the Rustin children were out on their own by the time Bayard graduated—Florence had left West Chester when Bayard was just a young child—the entire family was justifiably proud of his accomplishment. No one, however, was prouder than Julia. Ever the activist, she made appeals to organizations and influential people in the community in hope of finding a scholarship that would enable Bayard to go to college. When her appeals fell short, she turned to the African Methodist Episcopal (AME) Church, Janifer's church. An AME clergyman in Philadelphia used his influence to get Bayard a music scholarship to Wilberforce University. Wilberforce was an AME-sponsored school and one of the oldest black colleges in the United States.

As principal soloist for the Wilberforce Quartet, Bayard (far right) began what became an almost nomadic life of travel in support of one cause or another.

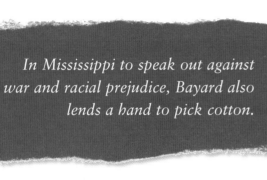

In Mississippi to speak out against war and racial prejudice, Bayard also lends a hand to pick cotton.

ALMOST AT ONCE, BAYARD BEGAN crisscrossing the country on behalf of the college. He was first tenor and principal soloist for the elite Wilberforce Quartet, which toured the country to raise money for the school. It was while at Wilberforce that he developed a passion for Negro spiritual songs. Later, after he transferred to Quaker-founded Cheyney State Teachers College, which was closer to home, he continued his travels, speaking to groups of other young college people about the Quaker beliefs in pacifism and nonviolence. Eventually, though, he was drawn to the bustling excitement of New York's Harlem, where he lived with his "sister" Bessie, a teacher in the public schools. He enrolled in classes at the City College of New York and later took a role in the chorus of the all-black Broadway musical *John Henry* to earn some money. When the show closed, he joined folk singer Josh White and His Carolinians to record an album. But it was his work for the Young Communist League (YCL), a student group that encouraged communism as it was practiced in Russia and which he joined while at the City College, that would truly cement his role as a political activist.

It was 1939, and Adolf Hitler had risen to power in Germany. The Japanese were rattling sabers in the East, having invaded China in 1937. The world was on the brink of World War II, and the United States was debating what role it would play in the conflict. The YCL sent Bayard to colleges around the country to speak out against war and racial injustice—two of the main positions it held and the reason Bayard found it ready-made for his Quaker upbringing and pacifist thinking. "[T]he Communists," he explained, ". . . appeared to be the only political organization expressing any concern about racial discrimination." Didn't Americans understand that if the money they planned to spend on weaponry and ammunition was spent instead on education and jobs, people—all people, poor blacks as well as poor whites—would be able to rise out of poverty? Didn't they understand that violence was not a solution? It led only to more violence. Didn't they understand that black people and white people and *all* people belonged to the same family?

And then he would sing a Negro spiritual so heartfelt and moving that it would leave his audiences weeping.

There is a balm in Gilead
To make the wounded whole;
There is a balm in Gilead
To heal the sin-sick soul.

If music is the universal language, Bayard understood that it also can help persuade. He often concluded his speaking engagements with a few moving gospel songs.

WHEN GERMANY INVADED RUSSIA IN 1941,

however, the YCL abruptly ended its campaign for Negro equality. Russia was worried that supporting a cause that was unpopular with the majority of white American policy makers would jeopardize any aid the United States might offer. Bayard felt betrayed by the YCL's turnabout, and he promptly ended his ties to the organization. Didn't anybody really care about the injustices heaped upon Negroes in America?

A. Philip Randolph cared, and Bayard volunteered his services to him.

As founder of the Brotherhood of Sleeping Car Porters, the first black labor union in the United States, Randolph was the most powerful and prominent black labor leader in the country. He was glad to have Bayard's help. He had recently demanded that President Franklin D. Roosevelt ban job discrimination in the defense industries as the United States geared up to supply weapons for the fight against Germany. Randolph also demanded that Roosevelt end Jim Crow segregation in the military, where whites and blacks were not allowed to serve side by side.

And when Roosevelt didn't act, Randolph planned the March on Washington to demonstrate how serious these issues were to black Americans. He asked Bayard to organize the march's youth division.

To Roosevelt, the threatened march felt like blackmail. He dug in his heels. How dare Randolph disrespect the president of the United States! Eleanor, Roosevelt's wife, didn't see it that way. She told the president that supporting Randolph's demands would be a good and honorable thing to do.

Less than a week before the scheduled July march, Roosevelt caved in and issued Executive Order 8802 ending racial discrimination in defense-industry jobs. It was only a partial victory, however, because it did nothing about segregation in the military. But having gained at least that much, Randolph cancelled the march as he had told the president he would.

Even though the 1941 March on Washington never took place, Bayard always believed it marked the beginning of the struggle for racial equality in the United States.

Asa Philip Randolph (1889–1979) became a mentor, father figure, and lifelong friend to Bayard.

19

FOLLOWING HIS WORK WITH RANDOLPH,
Bayard joined A. J. Muste's Fellowship of Reconciliation (FOR), a pacifist organization that opposed the participation of the United States in the conflict between Germany and its European neighbors. While he was in Indianapolis to deliver an FOR speech against involvement in the war, he stopped in at a small restaurant for a hamburger and was refused service. The proprietor explained that she could not serve him because whites would not enter a restaurant in which blacks were seated. Bayard was puzzled. He asked if she had any evidence that this was true. She didn't. So he suggested that they try an experiment. She would serve him a hamburger that he would leave untouched for fifteen minutes.

If, during that time, no whites entered the restaurant, he would leave.

Fifteen minutes later, several whites had entered the restaurant and ordered their meals. No one paid any attention to the young black man sitting by the front door with an uneaten lunch on his plate.

The woman brought Bayard a fresh, hot meal—and she continued to serve blacks after that. It was another small victory for racial equality.

Bayard in protest mode, passing out antiwar leaflets.

Although white bus riders could sit anywhere, Negroes were forbidden to sit forward of the row labeled White. Bayard was one of the first to voice outrage at this Jim Crow injustice.

THEN ON A TRIP FROM LOUISVILLE TO NASHVILLE in 1942, something happened.

Bayard boarded a bus and took the second seat. Seeing him, the driver told Bayard to move.

"Why?" Bayard asked.

"BECAUSE THAT'S THE LAW. NIGGERS RIDE IN BACK."

"I believe that I have a right to sit here," Bayard said.

He refused to move. The angry driver didn't know what to do except drive on.

And as Bayard sat there, things began to fester within him. He thought about the daily humiliations he had faced in West Chester when he was growing up. He thought of the late-night talk he'd heard about blacks being lynched in the South. He remembered those poor folks who would show up at his grandparents' house because they had nowhere else to turn. He thought life should not be so unjust!

How many more years were Negroes going to suffer such indignities?

Bayard considered the child sitting across from him. How many more years was that little white child going to suffer the injustice of thinking that blacks were inferior?

He became steadfast in his determination to remain in his seat.

At every stop, the bus driver repeated his demand.

At every stop, Bayard refused.

Sometimes life cooperated so completely! Bayard had long been reading about Mohandas K. Gandhi and his philosophy of direct nonviolent action in India's struggle for independence. Exasperated, the driver called ahead to the police and, just outside of Nashville, four officers dragged Bayard off the bus and began beating him.

Like Gandhi, Bayard did not resist. Instead, he shielded the blows. "There is no need to beat me," he calmly explained. "I am not resisting you."

His reaction seemed to confuse and frustrate his attackers. Where was the fight?

Then a few white passengers stepped up and demanded that the officers stop beating him. Giving up, the officers threw Bayard into their patrol car and took him to the station.

In Nashville, policemen tossed Bayard "from one to another like a volleyball." Then one of the white bus passengers showed up at the police station and spoke in Bayard's defense.

When Bayard met with the assistant district attorney, Ben West, to answer questions about the incident, West already had decided not to press charges. And as a sign of respect, he addressed Bayard as no black man was ever addressed in the South: "*Mister* Rustin."

As the United States geared up to enter World War II, Bayard protested not only the war but also the imprisonment of those who refused to join the military.

Bayard had made another small victory for Negro equality, and he vowed then and there to continue his crusade against injustice wherever he found it.

Stories of Bayard's activities and courage spread throughout the FOR. Before long, other pacifists convinced Muste to use some of the organization's energy to fight racial inequality using Gandhi's method of direct nonviolent action.

The Congress of Racial Equality—CORE—was born to challenge segregation.

MUSTE APPOINTED BAYARD to the staff of CORE, but that same year the United States entered World War II. Bayard received his notice to report for military duty a short time later. As a Quaker, Bayard could have been excused from military service because Quakers and others who belonged to religious groups that taught nonviolence were allowed to perform some other public service instead. But Bayard refused to join the military or do public service, his stance going beyond his deeply held religious belief that war was wrong. For him it was also a moral decision. Public service was not available to *all* who objected to the war—only to those whose objections were based on religious teaching. What about others who believed war was wrong? Public service wasn't available to them. What about the military's policy of racial segregation? Bayard believed it was "the basis of continuous violence."

He informed the draft board that he could not report for either military duty or public service and explained that his reasons for refusing all stemmed "from the basic spiritual truth that men are brothers in the sight of God" and that any practice "which separates man from his brother is evil and must be resisted.

"Though joyfully following the will of God, I regret that I must break the law of the State. I am prepared for whatever may follow." And once again, Julia and Janifer supported his decision.

What followed was federal prison in Ashland, Kentucky, where authorities regretted every minute of Bayard's presence. No sooner had he arrived at prison to serve his three-year sentence than Bayard began staging protests. He protested segregation in the prison system. He protested prisoners' living conditions. And he continued to study Gandhi. Prison officials begged for his transfer. For Bayard's part, he continued to disrupt the rigid prison routine—stopping only briefly when his grandfather died. Prison officials were unable to silence Bayard as they might have any other black inmate because he had influential friends like Randolph and Muste who checked on him. Eventually, prison officials won out, and he finished his sentence at Lewisburg, Pennsylvania. When he was released on June 11, 1946, officials were glad to be rid of him.

Oh freedom
Oh freedom
Oh freedom over me!

While serving his three-year prison sentence for refusing military service, Bayard taught himself to play the lute.

BAYARD PICKED UP EXACTLY WHERE HE LEFT OFF.

The U.S. Supreme Court had just ruled that Jim Crow segregation of bus passengers traveling from one state to another was illegal. With CORE's backing, Bayard and fifteen other men—eight blacks and eight whites working in teams of four—left on the Journey of Reconciliation to find out if the new law was being followed and to mount court challenges against those who weren't following it.

Bayard's team boarded a bus bound from Washington, D.C., in the spring of 1947. Two men— one black and one white—always sat up front in the section traditionally reserved for white passengers. Two others sat farther back. Things started out smoothly enough, but when they got to Chapel Hill, North Carolina, events took a sour turn. The bus driver called the police. The two Journeyers sitting in the front of the bus were dragged off and arrested. Bayard and his white partner, who had been sitting farther back in the bus, moved into the white section.

Again, the driver got the police.

All four men were sentenced to serve jail time for their acts of civil disobedience. CORE had planned to appeal the sentences but, unfortunately, the black lawyer it had entrusted with the ticket receipts claimed that they had been "lost." Had the lawyer been threatened with retaliation? Had he been paid to say the tickets were lost? No one is certain.

The judge in the case sentenced Bayard and his black colleague to thirty days on a chain gang. Their white partners received longer sentences because the conservative judge declared that Northern white liberals shouldn't upset the customs of the South. Although the sentences of the white Journeyers were later reduced, Bayard couldn't help but joke with them years later, "Well, you see, there was some advantages to being black."

Upon his release from prison in Lewisburg, Bayard returned to CORE and joined the Journey of Reconciliation. The Journeyers included, from the left, Worth Randle, Wally Nelson, Ernest Bromley, James Peck, Igal Roodenko, Rustin, Joe Felmet, George Houser, and Andrew Johnson.

Eventually, Negroes got fed up with unjust treatment. They got fed up with Jim Crow laws that made them second-class citizens. It was Thursday, December 1, 1955. The place was Montgomery, Alabama. Rosa Parks, a respected forty-two-year-old seamstress working with the NAACP, decided to test the legality of the Jim Crow laws that forced black riders to sit in the back of buses. She refused to give up her bus seat to a standing white man, and she was arrested. Black citizens were outraged, and their outrage didn't go unnoticed by the Women's Political Council, a group that worked to increase the political power of Montgomery's black community. It had often discussed a bus boycott as a method to end racial seating on Montgomery's buses, but the timing had never been right. With the arrest of Parks, however, the council moved into action. Jo Ann Robinson, head of the Women's Political Council, quickly produced thousands of leaflets that called for a one-day boycott of the city's bus system to protest racial seating and to strike a financial blow on the city; running empty buses would dig deep into city government's pockets. The following Monday—

THE DAY ROSA PARKS WENT TO COURT—

the Montgomery city buses were practically empty as black people walked to work, took cabs, or shared rides with those who owned cars.

It was the first large-scale mass protest against a segregation law in the history of the United States. And the one-day boycott grew into long-lasting community action while lawyers appealed the conviction of Rosa Parks.

Following her conviction for refusing to give up her bus seat to a standing white man, Rosa Parks is escorted to jail by her attorney and a deputy.

IN THE EARLY DAYS OF THE PROTEST, the black leadership formed the Montgomery Improvement Association to publicize the action and to raise money. E. D. Nixon, a local NAACP official and respected labor leader, asked the Reverend Dr. Martin Luther King, Jr., to serve as the association's spokesman. King, at first, declined, believing that he was too new to town and too young at twenty-six to take on such responsibility. But Nixon persisted and the minister from the Dexter Avenue Baptist Church eventually agreed.

Things quickly turned nasty. White segregationists bombed King's home. Two nights later, a bomb exploded in Nixon's yard. Montgomery was on the verge of a full-scale racial war. A. Philip Randolph asked Bayard, the expert on nonviolent action, to go to Montgomery to make sure that the protest remained peaceful and dignified.

In the years following his 1947 conviction in North Carolina, Bayard had continued to study Gandhi's techniques of peaceful, nonviolent protest while he appealed his thirty-day sentence to a chain gang. He also traveled abroad, organizing the Free India Committee to help in that struggling nation's efforts to become independent from Great Britain. He had hoped to meet Gandhi, who was leading his nation to independence, but he did not get to India until 1949, and Gandhi was assassinated before Bayard's arrival. He regretted not getting to meet Gandhi, but 1949 held another disappointment: the North

Carolina Supreme Court ruled against his appeal to have his sentence overturned. He surrendered his freedom in March 1949, and wrote about his experiences on the chain gang in articles in the *New York Post*. The articles had such an impact that North Carolina outlawed chain gangs within two years of their publication. In the early

In the years following his North Carolina conviction, Bayard protested French nuclear testing in the Sahara and also lent his support to independence efforts in India (above) and Africa (opposite).

32

1950s he continued with his international efforts, working to assist African nations with their independence because he believed, like Randolph, that independence and economic opportunity were the keys to peace.

Although Bayard had misgivings about going to Montgomery—he didn't want to appear to be a Northern outsider sticking his nose into Southern business—he couldn't refuse Randolph. He arrived in Montgomery on Tuesday, February 21, 1956. That same day the courts charged more than one hundred leaders of the protest with violating Alabama's law against boycotts. The charges were meant to spread fear and to end the protest. Borrowing from Gandhi's philosophy, Bayard suggested that everyone charged should put on their Sunday best and turn themselves in rather than wait for the sheriff to arrest them like criminals.

The action had the desired effect. White community leaders didn't know what to think while, Bayard said,

"NEGROES WERE THRILLED TO SEE THEIR LEADERS SURRENDER WITHOUT BEING HUNTED DOWN."

MEANWHILE, BAYARD BUSIED HIMSELF. While sitting in his motel room, he composed lyrics for a freedom song. He wrote drafts of many of King's speeches, as well as the first article, "Our Struggle," that ever appeared under King's name. He suggested ideas to keep the protest on the nation's front pages. He ran workshops on nonviolent action, speaking at length with King about Gandhi's philosophy and methods.

Bayard became King's teacher.

When he had arrived in Montgomery, he had found armed guards patrolling outside King's house. King himself had applied for a permit to carry a weapon in his car and had guns inside his house. Bayard insisted that a protest could not be truly nonviolent if there were weapons, and the protest leader had to be the model of nonviolence.

King listened. He learned. And the weapons and armed guards were removed.

We are moving on to vict'ry
With hope and dignity.
We shall all stand together
Till every one is free.

We know love is the watchword
For peace and liberty.
Black and white, all are brothers
To live in harmony.

As an expert in nonviolent action, Bayard went to Montgomery, Alabama, to advise the bus boycott's leaders, the Reverend Ralph Abernathy (far left) and the Reverend Dr. Martin Luther King, Jr., among others, in the methods of peaceful protest.

Following the Montgomery bus boycott, Bayard became teacher and trusted adviser to the Reverend Dr. Martin Luther King, Jr., until Dr. King's assassination in 1968.

THREE HUNDRED EIGHTY-ONE DAYS AFTER IT BEGAN, the Montgomery bus boycott triumphed. The nine justices of the U.S. Supreme Court finally heard the case against Rosa Parks and ruled that segregation—racial seating—on the Montgomery buses was unconstitutional. And riders returned to the buses.

Bayard encouraged King to build on the energy of the Montgomery bus boycott by forming an organization that would continue nonviolent protests of segregation laws and practices across the country. But King didn't have time to set up an organization. So along with Ella Baker and Stanley Levison—two other prominent civil rights workers—Bayard organized what became the Southern Christian Leadership Conference (SCLC), and King became its leader.

From the platform of the SCLC and with Bayard's guidance, King became one of the leading voices for nonviolence in twentieth-century America. He would continue to seek Bayard's advice for the rest of his life. Bayard, for his part in the Montgomery bus boycott, sought no fanfare—perhaps echoing a poem he wrote while still in high school:

I ask of you no shining gold;
I seek not epitaph or fame;
No monument of stone for me,
For man need never speak my name.

FOLLOWING THE VICTORY IN MONTGOMERY,

protests and boycotts wracked the South and other parts of the United States. Sit-ins modeled on Bayard's early restaurant protests took place. Freedom Riders, similar to those of the Journey of Reconciliation, boarded buses. Pickets demonstrated at public pools and theaters, and Negroes entered white-only bathrooms and department-store dressing rooms. And they sent their children to white-only schools and then filed lawsuits when their children were barred from entering.

In 1960 a fresh decade dawned, and John F. Kennedy was elected president. He had campaigned to bring about black equality but had failed during the first years of his presidency to deliver on that promise. After years of protests that followed the Montgomery bus boycott, A. Philip Randolph believed that the mood in the country was right for a large-scale, nonviolent protest in Washington, D.C.

NOT EVERYONE AGREED.

Kennedy finally had a strong civil rights bill before Congress in 1963 that would make racial discrimination in public places, such as restaurants, theaters, and hotels, illegal. It also made racial discrimination in employment illegal and tried to deal with the problem of denying blacks their right to vote in the South. Kennedy was afraid that a mass protest would reflect badly on him and might derail the legislation. Several black leaders also believed that the timing was not right. But since the Montgomery bus boycott, the white power structure in the South had dug in, and white segregationists had turned bolder and more violent. Randolph convinced the other black leaders that the time was now or never, and he chose a date: Wednesday, August 28. The timing in August had no particular significance, but the year most certainly did; the Emancipation Proclamation had been signed in 1863, and in the one hundred years since, Negroes in the United States had noticed little improvement in their lives. Randolph asked Bayard to organize the protest.

Protests, such as this lunch-counter sit-in, wracked the South and many other parts of the United States following the success of the Montgomery bus boycott.

to organize the March on Washington for Jobs and Freedom.

He set to work in a crowded office in Harlem. His dedication and energy inspired his small staff, and together they planned for every eventuality. Extra planes, trains, and buses were scheduled to bring in marchers from every part of the country. How many blankets would they need for protesters who arrived the night before the march? How many portable toilets should they have on hand? How many parking spaces would they need for buses and automobiles? Nothing was left to chance.

Bayard and his assistant, Cleveland Robinson, advertise the March on Washington for Jobs and Freedom outside their Harlem office on West 130th Street.

Bayard even told people what to bring in their box lunches! And fearing that uniformed police might spell trouble, he arranged for off-duty black police officers from up and down the East Coast to patrol the march out of uniform and without weapons. On top of all this, he had to organize a program that would both inspire and entertain what he promised would be one hundred thousand marchers under Washington's August sun. Privately, he thought that twice that many people might possibly show up, but he told his staff not to mention it to reporters. Reporters were always eager to announce failure.

Bayard points at a map of the route that marchers will take in the 1963 March on Washington for Jobs and Freedom. The poster on the wall in the background was used on the cover of the march's souvenir program.

WEDNESDAY DAWNED.

Bayard strolled over to the Washington Monument to see how the march was shaping up. Journalists and the security patrol greeted him, but there were only a handful of protesters. When someone asked where the crowds were, Bayard momentarily felt his stomach knot.

But ever unflappable, he pulled a piece of paper out of his pocket and checked it against his pocket watch. "Gentlemen, everything is going according to Hoyle," he reported.

Rachelle Horowitz, an assistant who was walking beside him, was shocked. The scrap of paper was blank!

By nine thirty, though, a crowd of forty thousand people had gathered. By eleven, police reported that nearly one hundred thousand had assembled and that all roads leading to Washington were clogged with buses and cars.

On the morning of August 28, 1963, buses squeezed into a parking area near the Washington Monument, and protesters flocked to the grassy slopes that surround it.

By eleven o'clock, a crowd of nearly one hundred thousand had assembled in the area where earlier Bayard had found only a handful of people.

43

And around midday the crowd marched.

A quarter million men, women, and children. A quarter million blacks and whites of all faiths and beliefs. A quarter million united in a single purpose marched to the Lincoln Memorial to demonstrate their grievances.

At the end of a program that included opera singer Marian Anderson, A. Philip Randolph, gospel singer Mahalia Jackson, and the NAACP's Roy Wilkins, among others, the Reverend Dr. Martin Luther King, Jr., held the audience spellbound, as Bayard knew only he could, when he spoke of his dream of a United States that lived up to its promise that "all men are created equal."

The march was "one of those few moments in American history when there was almost absolute unity within the black community." It also proved that we were capable of being one people.

One people. One family. Just as Julia had taught him so long ago.

> *Free at last, free at last*
> *I thank God I'm free at last.*

Left: A quarter million people marched from the Washington Monument to the Lincoln Memorial, actually setting out before they were scheduled. Bayard joked that he had to hustle the march leaders so they could catch up with their followers! Inset: At the end of the program, the Reverend Dr. Martin Luther King, Jr., moved the crowd as only he could.

The rest of his life would change little. He would continue his work to bring dignity and equality to the oppressed wherever he found them, believing that when freedom was challenged and when people were treated unjustly, he had an obligation to do something about it.

He always had. He always would.

That was Bayard!

The remainder of Bayard's life was spent speaking out against injustice wherever he found it.

> *We are all one. And if we don't know it, we will learn it the hard way.*
> —Bayard Rustin

Author's Note

WHEN I FIRST SAW BAYARD RUSTIN'S NAME, it was in a footnote—almost an afterthought, as if the author felt an obligation to mention his name but at the same time didn't want to draw too much attention to it. Then I read that more than ten years before Rosa Parks's historic refusal to surrender her bus seat, Bayard also had refused to move to the Jim Crow section of the bus on which he was riding. Why had one received such public attention and the other practically none at all? I was immediately curious.

Like most people, I knew very little about Bayard. As I began researching his life, though, I came to realize that his is just the sort of story I like telling—an underdog, an outsider, someone who hasn't received his or her just recognition from society.

Yet, Bayard Rustin played a major role in the twentieth-century fight for African American civil rights in the United States—but always as an adviser to the leadership, an organizer who remained largely invisible. Despite his talents and skills, he was (and is) a controversial figure. This was largely because he briefly belonged to the Young Communist League, as had many of his generation; he was a war objector who chose prison over serving in the military or doing alternative service, even after the bombing of Pearl Harbor; and he was a homosexual. Some

Left to right: Bayard at a press conference at Freedom House, an organization that promotes democracy around the world; a rally for voting rights in Alabama; with young refugees as part of the International Rescue Committee; and with Prime Minister Golda Meir (1898–1978) as a show of support for Israel.

African American leaders found in Bayard Rustin an activist who was also a liability, and they jockeyed to keep him in the background. Indeed, even some of his friends—like the Reverend Dr. Martin Luther King, Jr., who often sought his advice—abandoned him when it was expedient to do so. In 1960, an election year, A. Philip Randolph, King, and Rustin had planned for mass protests at the conventions of the two major political parties. However, Adam Clayton Powell, Jr., Harlem's powerful African American congressman, feared that any demonstrating at the conventions would cost him his influence in Congress. He threatened to announce that King and Bayard had a homosexual relationship. The charge was untrue, but to spare King any embarrassment, Bayard offered to resign from his position as King's assistant and director of the SCLC's New York office. Bayard fully expected King to stand up to Powell and refuse the resignation, but King disliked uncomfortable situations and did no such thing. Even so, Bayard never held a grudge. He was content being an organizer and worker behind the scenes, and he continued in an unofficial capacity to advise King until King's assassination.

Bayard was a man of many dimensions—an intellectual, an organizer, a speaker, a singer, a stage actor, an artist, and a collector. Yet, it was his social activism and his use of Gandhian methods of nonviolence that most interested me. Seemingly without fear, he fought for the dignity of an entire people knowing that every time he stood for his beliefs, it could—and likely would—mean a brutal beating or an arrest or both. He sat in at lunch counters long before the emergence of organized sit-ins. He made the first freedom ride, upon which later Freedom Rides were modeled. During a lifetime of direct nonviolent confrontation, he was arrested more than twenty times for acts of civil disobedience. It is little wonder that he has been called the "intellectual engineer" of the civil rights movement.

Bayard was born in West Chester, Pennsylvania, in 1912, and—dissatisfied with the status quo—he began to protest racial injustice in the 1930s and 1940s. It was a courageous and daring thing for an African American man to do, given the pervasive prejudice at the time. He attended three different colleges, but he never earned a degree from any of them. When he settled in Harlem, he landed a part in the short-lived stage production of *John Henry*, starring Paul Robeson. Later, to earn money, he sang with Josh White and His Carolinians and recorded an album of songs with them. But always, it was social activism—especially with regard to racial injustices—that was his true calling.

Bayard was fifty-one years old when the success of the March on Washington for Jobs and Freedom (1963) thrust him upon the world stage. In the years following the march, he would lend his voice to help refugees, assist fledgling democracies around the globe, monitor elections, speak out against apartheid, and always—*always*—support the unjustly treated. At the time of his death on August 24, 1987, Bayard had been awarded eighteen honorary degrees from colleges and universities in recognition of his life's work of compassion. His was a life marked by self-sacrifice and but one intolerance—injustice.

To be true to the times in which Bayard lived, and with the greatest respect, I referred to African Americans as colored, black, and Negro in this book. These were the terms that Bayard used to refer to himself and others of his race.

Many different sources were used as references, and I am indebted to those who told Bayard's story before me. Of course, I am most grateful to Bayard himself for living the life he lived. But I am also thankful to him for *Down the Line: The Collected Writings of Bayard Rustin; Strategies for Freedom: The Changing Patterns of Black Protest*; and "The Reminiscences of Bayard Rustin," Columbia University Oral History Project, interview with Ed Edwin. Several other titles were indispensable: *Bayard Rustin and the Civil Rights Movement* by Daniel Levine; *Lost Prophet: The Life and Times of Bayard Rustin* by John D'Emilio; *Bayard Rustin: Troubles I've Seen* by Jervis Anderson; and *Time on Two Crosses: The Collected Writings of Bayard Rustin*, edited by Devon W. Carbado and Donald Weise.

For young readers wanting to know more about Bayard's remarkable life, I suggest *Bayard Rustin: Behind the Scenes of the Civil Rights Movement* by James Haskins. Also, I highly recommend *Brother Outsider: The Life of Bayard Rustin*, a short film by Nancy Kates and Bennett Singer.

Finally, I thank Dina Robinson of California Newsreel for bending rules that allowed me to purchase and view *Brother Outsider: The Life of Bayard Rustin*; Courtney Smith and Elizabeth Grefrath of Columbia University's Oral History Research Office for rushing me "The Reminiscences of Bayard Rustin"; Pamela C. Powell, photo archivist, Chester County Historical Society; and Walter Naegle of the Bayard Rustin Fund, Inc., and Bayard's long-time partner.

The architects of the 1963 March on Washington for Jobs and Freedom, A. Philip Randolph and Bayard Rustin, on the cover of Life *magazine.*

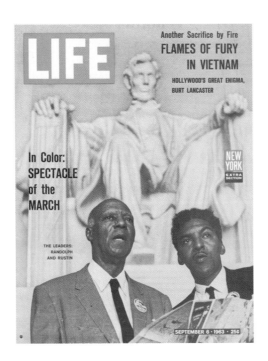

The inimitable Bayard Rustin, Trafalgar Square in London, 1983.